MW00413872

SCORPIO

~SUN SIGN SERIES~

ALSO BY JOANNA MARTINE WOOLFOLK

Sexual Astrology

Honeymoon for Life

The Only Astrology Book You'll Ever Need

SCORPIO

~SUN SIGN SERIES~
JOANNA MARTINE WOOLFOLK

TAYLOR TRADE PUBLISHING
LANHAM • NEW YORK • BOULDER • TORONTO • PLYMOUTH, UK

Published by Taylor Trade Publishing
An imprint of The Rowman & Littlefield Publishing Group, Inc.
4501 Forbes Boulevard, Suite 200, Lanham, Maryland 20706
www.rlpgtrade.com

Estover Road, Plymouth PL6 7PY, United Kingdom

Distributed by National Book Network

Copyright © 2011 by Joanna Martine Woolfolk

All rights reserved. No part of this book may be reproduced in any form or by any electronic
or mechanical means, including information storage and retrieval systems, without written
permission from the publisher, except by a reviewer who may quote passages in a review.

British Library Cataloguing in Publication Information Available

Library of Congress Cataloging-in-Publication Data

Woolfolk, Joanna Martine.
   Scorpio / Joanna Martine Woolfolk.
      p. cm.—(Sun sign series)
   ISBN 978-1-58979-560-0 (pbk. : alk. paper)—ISBN 978-1-58979-535-8 (electronic)
   1. Scorpio (Astrology) I. Title.
   BF1727.5.W66 2011
   133.5'273—dc22   2011003351

♾™ The paper used in this publication meets the minimum requirements of American
National Standard for Information Sciences—Permanence of Paper for Printed Library
Materials, ANSI/NISO Z39.48-1992.

Printed in the United States of America

I dedicate this book to the memory of
William Woolfolk
whose wisdom continues to guide me,

and to
James Sgandurra
who made everything bloom again.

CONTENTS

ABOUT THE AUTHOR

Astrologer Joanna Martine Woolfolk has had a long career as an author, columnist, lecturer, and counselor. She has written the monthly horoscope for numerous magazines in the United States, Europe, and Latin America—among them *Marie Claire*, *Harper's Bazaar*, *Redbook*, *Self*, *YM*, *House Beautiful*, and *StarScroll International*. In addition to the best-selling *The Only Astrology Book You'll Ever Need*, Joanna is the author of *Sexual Astrology*, which has sold over a million copies worldwide, and *Astrology Source*, an interactive CD-ROM.

Joanna is a popular television and radio personality who has been interviewed by Barbara Walters, Regis Philbin, and Sally Jessy Raphael. She has appeared in a regular astrology segment on *New York Today* on NBC-TV and on *The Fairfield Exchange* on

CT Cable Channel 12, and she appears frequently on television and radio shows around the country. You can visit her website at www.joannamartinewoolfolk.com.

ACKNOWLEDGMENTS

Many people contribute to the creation of a book, some with ideas and editorial suggestions, and some unknowingly through their caring and love.

Among those who must know how much they helped is Jed Lyons, the elegant, erudite president of my publishers, the Rowman & Littlefield Publishing Group. Jed gave me the idea for this Sun Sign series, and I am grateful for his faith and encouragement.

Enormous gratitude also to Michael K. Dorr, my literary agent and dear friend, who has believed in me since we first met and continues to be my champion. I thank Michael for his sharp editor's eye and imbuing me with confidence.

Two people who don't know how much they give are my beloved sister and brother, Patricia G. Reynhout and Dr. John T. Galdamez. They sustain me with their unfailing devotion and support.

*We are born at a given moment, in a given place,
and like vintage years of wine, we have the
qualities of the year and of the season
in which we are born.*

CARL GUSTAV JUNG

INTRODUCTION

When my publishers suggested I write a book devoted solely to Scorpio, I was thrilled. I've long wanted to concentrate exclusively on your wonderful sign. You are very special in the zodiac. Astrology teaches that Scorpio is the sign of regeneration and rebirthing. Your sign represents passion, transformation, life force, and the power of creation. You carry deep personal strength and are remarkable in both physical and emotional energy. You're creative, protective, spiritual, ambitious, intuitive, and intense in your feelings. Karmic teachers say you were specially picked to be a Scorpio because you were a healer and great spiritual teacher in a previous life. But whether or not one believes in past lives, in *this* life you are Scorpio, the towering spirit of change, renewal, resurgence, and new beginnings.

These days it has become fashionable to be a bit dismissive of Sun signs (the sign that the Sun was in at the time of your birth). Some people sniff that "everyone knows about Sun signs." They say the descriptions are too cookie-cutter, too much a cardboard figure, too inclusive (how can every Scorpio be the same?).

Of course every Scorpio is not the same! And many of these differences not only are genetic and environmental, but are differences in your *charts*. Another Scorpio would not necessarily have your Moon sign, or Venus sign, or Ascendant. However, these are factors to consider later—after you have studied your Sun sign. (In *The Only Astrology Book You'll Ever Need*, I cover in depth differences in charts: different Planets, Houses, Ascendants, etc.)

First and foremost, you are a Scorpio. Scorpio is the sign the Sun was traveling through at the time of your birth.* The Sun is our most powerful planet. (In astrological terms, the Sun is referred to as a planet even though technically it is a "luminary.") It gives us life, warmth, energy, food. It is the force that sustains us on Earth. The Sun is also the most important and pervasive influence in your horoscope and in many ways determines how others see you. Your Sun sign governs your individuality, your distinctive style, and your drive to fulfill your goals.

Your sign of Scorpio symbolizes the role you are given to play in this life. It's as if at the moment of your birth you were pushed onstage into a drama called *This Is My Life*. In this drama, you are the starring actor—and Scorpio is the character you play. What aspects of this character are you going to project? The Scorpio willpower, profundity, and persistence? Its ability to understand and to heal, to form lasting relationships? Or its obsessiveness and vindictiveness, ruthlessness, and dictatorial ways? Your sign of Scorpio describes your journey through this life, for it is your task to evolve into a perfect Scorpio.

For each of us, the most interesting, most gripping subject is *self*. The longer I am an astrologer—which at this point is half my lifetime—the more I realize that what we all want to know about is ourselves. "Who am I?" you ask. You want to know what makes

---

*From our viewpoint here on Earth, the Sun travels around the Earth once each year. Within the space of that year, the Sun moves through all twelve signs of the zodiac, spending approximately one month in each sign.

you tick, why you have such intense feelings, and whether others are also insecure. People ask me questions like, "What kind of man should I look for?" "Why am I discontented with my job?" or "The man I'm dating is a Capricorn; will we be happy together?" They ask me if they'll ever find true love and when they will get out of a period of sadness or fear or the heavy burden of problems. They ask about their path in life and how they can find more fulfillment.

So I continue to see that the reason astrology exists is to answer questions about you. Basically, it's all about *you*. Astrology has been described as a stairway leading into your deeper self. It holds out the promise that you do not have to pass through life reacting blindly to experience, that you can within limits direct your own destiny and in the process reach a truer self-understanding.

Astrologically, the place to begin the study of yourself is your Sun sign. In this book, you'll read about your many positive qualities as well as your Scorpio issues and negative inclinations. You'll find insights into your power and potentials, advice about love and sex, career guidance, health and diet tips, and information about myriads of objects, places, concepts, and things to which Scorpio is attached. You'll also find topics not usually included in other astrology books—such as how Scorpio fits in with Chinese astrology and with numerology.

Come with me on this exploration of the "infinite variety" (in Shakespeare's phrase) of being a Scorpio.

Joanna Martine Woolfolk
Stamford, Connecticut
June 2011

SCORPIO

OCTOBER 23–NOVEMBER 21

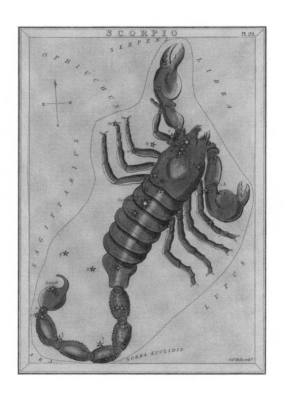

SCORPIO

Pl. 23.

OPHIUCHUS

SERPENS

LIBRA

SAGITTARIUS

LUPUS

ARA

NORMA EUCLIDIS

PART ONE

ALL ABOUT YOU

ILLUMINATING QUOTATIONS

"Every act of creation is first an act of destruction."

—Pablo Picasso, artist, a Scorpio

"Dying is an art, like everything else. I do it exceptionally well."

—Sylvia Plath, author, a Scorpio

"Here we are, trapped in the amber of the moment. There is no why."

—Kurt Vonnegut, author, a Scorpio

"Somewhere, something incredible is waiting to be known."

—Carl Sagan, astronomer and astrophysicist, a Scorpio

"In the depth of winter I finally learned that there was in me an invincible summer."

—Albert Camus, philosopher and author, a Scorpio

"Rage, rage against the dying of the light."

—Dylan Thomas, poet, a Scorpio

YOUR SCORPIO PERSONALITY

....

YOUR MOST LIKEABLE TRAIT: Idealism

....

The bright side of Scorpio: Imaginative, determined, ambitious,
    perceptive, idealistic, intensely able to nurture
The dark side of Scorpio: Obstinate, secretive, resentful, jealous,
    domineering, compulsive

*Scorpio represents the force of life through its cycles of change
and regeneration—birth, life, sex, death, and rebirth. As a Scorpio,
you are passionate about everything that captures your interest,
whether this is pursuing an ambition, doing creative work, expand-
ing your knowledge, accumulating financial gain, fostering relationships, blending into sexual unions. In all you do, you dig beneath
the surface to find the essential "heart of the matter." You search
for an intense experience of life. However, you are also controlled
and controlling, and extremely careful about opening the least bit of
vulnerability. Although you seek connections on the deepest level,
you also stand apart.*

This is the sign of extremes. Scorpio people are variously described as powerful, weak, independent, clinging, passionate, and

cold. Clearly, you are a bundle of contradictions encompassing the best and worst in human nature.

The key to your personality is intensity. You do nothing by half-measures. Magnetic, emotional, capable of exerting tremendous force, your strength is hidden in the depths. In the sign of Scorpio, the element of Water is Fixed, an image that suggests an iceberg or a bottomless well. You may appear impassive, sometimes unapproachable, but turbulent passions are always roiling underneath, invisible on the surface.

You live on many levels. While you present a smiling face of calm control to the world, you're ferociously persistent and extremely strong-willed. People have difficulty reading you because you exercise such great self-discipline. Yet you're also flexible when it comes to working out solutions. Confronted with a disaster, you absolutely will not accept defeat. With single-minded concentration, you set to work solving the problem. And with your great adaptability, you're extremely agile in sidestepping obstacles and figuring out a dozen new ways to get to your goal. In a wonderful paradox, flexibility is one of your most effective methods of controlling situations. You can quickly channel your awesome energies into new paths and, if you must, embark on an entirely different course.

Because of its complications and complexities, Scorpio is the most misunderstood sign in the zodiac. Yours is a convoluted mind, linked to mystery, sex, power, and intrigue. Basically, you always have a hidden agenda. You're someone of incredible depth and brilliance, and your inner psyche is a labyrinth of wheels within wheels, boxes within boxes. Even when you seem to be at ease and relaxed, you are always evaluating, figuring out your moves, working out strategy.

Much of this has to do with control, which is what you are all about. For Scorpio, being out of control is being in psychic danger—only when you control are you safe. Nothing is worse than to feel swept away by outside forces, though you must also struggle against powerful *inner* forces that threaten to rule you. Thus, self-mastery is definitely your lifelong task.

Your Scorpio evolution is the journey toward controlling in *positive* ways: putting order into chaotic situations, being of use to others and therefore meeting an unfulfilled need, arranging your personal environment so it works smoothly for you. The unevolved Scorpio tries to control other people and manipulate situations for its own greed. As you can see, the forces of light and dark continually oppose each other in your turbulent psyche.

What you need is to transmute your fervor into positive relationships and meaningful work. It is very easy to waste yourself on what is unworthy of you, and then your feelings turn inward, become imprisoned, at times even destructive. More than natives of any other sign, Scorpios live at a high pitch of emotion. Its negative aspects are brooding, jealousy, resentment, even vengefulness. The positive aspect is your unswerving commitment once your emotions are engaged. The Scorpion energy, drive, and endurance are legendary. Above all, you seek to give your life a meaningful pattern, to find a deeper purpose.

The complexity of your mind makes it difficult for you to skim the surface. You have unquenchable curiosity and a tenacious memory, and whether you're studying a new subject, learning a language, hunting down a fact, or just reading for entertainment, there is a quality of penetration to the way you think. You also have a philosophical turn of mind and may become interested in religion and the occult. Your sixth sense enables you to intuit things before they happen.

All the Water signs (Cancer, Scorpio, Pisces) tend to be psychic, but you, Scorpio, delve into the powers of the mind that others are afraid of. In a sense, you're a psychic detective, forever digging into reasons why, wanting to know the answer to the deepest questions. Yours is the zodiacal sign of birth, sex, death, and regeneration— areas of human existence in which a person confronts the mysteries of the universe. Many Scorpio natives are brilliant doctors, surgeons, scientists, and spiritual leaders. Jonas Salk, Christian Barnard, Carl Sagan, Marie Curie, and Martin Luther are among them.

Your finest attributes—and your worst—are revealed in relationships. Certainly, one of your great strengths is your loyalty in relationships. Yours is a Fixed sign, and you are ever steadfast. For family, friends, lover, and mate you're a Rock of Gibraltar. Scorpio is the one who loves longest. Come hell or high water, you hang on.

But always with Scorpio, relationships are complicated. This is not surprising when you consider that you can be simultaneously generous and affectionate, violent and unpredictable; in your sunniest moods, there is always a hint of an imminent change in the weather. You are deeply loyal but also intensely jealous and possessive. You cannot tolerate the thought that anyone you love might have a yearning, or even a simple yen, for anyone else. With you, it's all or nothing at all. Moderation, restraint, and certainly *casual* are not in your emotional vocabulary.

You never forget a kindness and will try to repay it handsomely. Conversely, you never forgive an injury and will wait years to get even. In fact, most of the time, getting even isn't enough—you want vengeance. It is strictly not advisable to do harm to any Scorpion. You make a dangerous enemy, for you are as subtle and deadly as the symbol of your sign.

You are a fierce competitor, though often you manage to conceal this from others. You file away pieces of information, facts, and names, and don't hesitate to use what you know if the occasion arises. When you spot a weakness in a rival, you move in quickly for the kill. In business, you accomplish things first and announce them second. By the time an opponent is aware of your progress, it is a fait accompli.

Your nature makes you subject to obsessive drives that can be resistant to reason. You will dominate and control anyone who lets you. Suspicious and wary, you are reluctant to trust your heart to anyone. But once you do, you love deeply.

In describing the sign of Scorpio, too many astrologers forget to emphasize how generous, kind, devoted, even gentle a Scorpio can be. Many idealists who adhere to high principles are born under this sign. Blessed with a native understanding of the human heart, you understand the problems and pain of others and have an almost magical ability to help others see their own strengths. In the zodiac, you are known as a healer.

What all Scorpios have in common is intensity of feeling. You are torn between emotion and reason, but in the end it is emotion that rules you—not only rules you, but characterizes you. You put the whole force of your personality behind whatever you do. You are passionate in love, and passionate about everything in which you become involved: work, relationships, hobbies, causes. You're an individual painted in vivid colors; there is no such thing as a pastel Scorpio.

THE INNER YOU

You have great strength, determination, and willpower. But no matter how calm and cool you appear on the outside, you've got a well of seething emotions underneath. For the most part, though, you keep your intensity under control by channeling it into useful activities. You're a high achiever, and you seem to "get" things in a flash—with powerful psychic feelings, you've learned to trust. When you latch onto a new opportunity, you explore it in great depth before going ahead. Deep inside you is a gladiator spirit, and if you channel this fighting energy into positive goals (your continuing lesson), you will always be one of life's great winners. At times, however, you feel you are a lone warrior in a harsh world. You're a complex person who can't always express how you feel, but one thing is certain: The things you want, you want badly.

HOW OTHERS SEE YOU

It's probably your secretiveness that makes people so interested in finding out what you think. You're often the guru in a group, the one with uncanny hunches about the future and piercing insights into other people's motivations. Many believe that even your humor contains the barb of truth. People are aware of your reputation for sensuality and fantasize about you as a lover. You're frequently viewed as overly controlling and too ambitious—even power-hungry—but also as someone who can be trusted because you never make false promises.

GUARD AGAINST:
Allowing Your Dark Self to Take Over

You're subject to moodiness that creeps up and ambushes you from behind. You pull your feelings inward and keep silent. You brood about slights and hurts, hold on to grudges, obsess, and then push down your anger until it turns into indefinable depression. Scorpio has the capacity to feel deeply and intensely, and, basically, you need to guard against being engulfed by your emotions.

You're the sign of secrets; your negativity and fears are layered and complicated. On the surface, you seem charming and gregarious, but you isolate yourself emotionally from others. You feel the loneliness, but your lack of trust prevents you from communicating openly and forming connections. The only way to combat more and more emotional seclusion is to speak of your feelings. Spoken words are different from thought words, and hearing yourself speak will make you *hear* your feelings for the first time. You will gain insight and comfort. This takes trusting another person with your "secrets," but even small steps of disclosure will release you from inner demons.

Yours is the sign of death and rebirthing; you go through many cycles of renewal in your lifetime. The point of being born a Scorpio is to learn to evolve, transform, and express your deep love, creativity, nurturing, and brilliance. And this will happen only when you're courageous enough to talk about what you are feeling.

YOUR GREATEST CHALLENGE:
To Learn Positive Ways in Which to Control

Control is the word that defines Scorpio. People born under other signs may be driven by ambition, ego, the need to be taken care of, or something else, but you need to exercise control so that you'll be safe. In a sense, you operate as a warrior in the midst of a hostile, chaotic world—and the only way to protect yourself from harm is to exercise complete control and put up impenetrable defenses. From an early age, you learn to manipulate people and scenarios. You obtain valuable knowledge, make useful connections, and squirrel away information to pull out when threatened. You know how to push emotional buttons and stage-manage others into doing what you want.

Another way you control is by squashing your own emotional responses so that you don't feel pain, abandonment, hurt. If you control the *inside* forces, you can deal with outside forces. Therefore, you cut yourself off from feelings and sublimate your strong emotions into intense career drives, or sexual exploits, or even destructive acting out (drinking, drugs). You show nothing on the surface, and people see you as either easy to deal with or cold as ice.

Your great challenge, Scorpio, is to use your awesome personal power to control in ways that are healthy, productive, give you a sense of accomplishment, and create security. For example, keeping an organized home, taking care that your financial accounts are in order, staying on top of scheduling, making sure every aspect of work for which you're responsible is done to your best ability.

Control—when it doesn't manipulate others and is used in positive ways—is a beautiful thing. It keeps you happy and disciplined, gives you freedom, and insures that you live a fulfilled life.

YOUR ALTER EGO

Astrology gives us many tools in our lives to help manage our struggles and solve problems. One of these tools is to reach into your opposite sign in the zodiac—your polarity. For you, Scorpio, this is Taurus, sign of money, possessions, values, and being grounded in the things of the earth. Taurus people try to create a life of total stability. Like you, they have a deep need for security, but they don't become enmeshed in an obscure and seething inner world. Taurus focuses on the simple verities of close, intimate relationships, luxurious possessions, plenty of money in the bank, good food, and good sex.

Much as you may want all these things, as a Scorpio you tend to get caught in a vortex of more complicated desires. You want to stay safe by controlling what other people do. You can become obsessive about what can go wrong and try to alter the course of a situation. You long for deep sexual merging yet put up barriers to anyone getting that near to you emotionally.

Taurus, on the other hand, sees no point in wasting energy on what cannot be changed. The Taurus person concentrates on what works, on practicality and use. The Taurus nature is to plant strong roots (family, career) and build something he or she can depend on.

Both Taurus and Scorpio are Fixed signs and share the quality of holding on. Taurus holds on to what it owns (possessions, relationships), which can cause pain enough if Taurus loses anything. Yet Taurus ultimately takes comfort in its stolid, it-is-what-it-is attitude. You, Scorpio, hold on to your intense feelings about a particular outcome, person, idea, project. Indeed, you hold on to the *pain* of a rejection, insult, failure, or loss. Scorpio carries around a great deal of darkness to which you become resigned.

By tapping into Taurus's equanimity and steadiness, its placid approach to problems, you can ease your secret distress (e.g., guilt, obsession, mistrust). You can also benefit from Taurus's ability to make heartfelt connections. When you open your heart with trust instead of fear of being taken advantage of, you immediately begin to heal inner loneliness. You can also tap into Taurus's sociability and appreciation of beauty to bring pleasure and artistic expression into your life.

In turn, Taurus can learn from you how to see deeper, to look past a person's social status and material success and recognize another's heart. Taurus can be simplistic and superficial in its assessments, and needs your spiritual insight. Taurus can also profit from discovering how Scorpio inner-will can accomplish anything and against any odds. Certainly, the Scorpio force of courage is a major life lesson. And finally, Taurus needs to learn from you how to move through transformation and the process of reinvention—your phoenix ability to rise out of a dying self (whatever situation may be dying) and give birth to a new beginning.

SCORPIO IN LOVE

Sexual magnetism defines Scorpio. You give off an enticing air of mystery, a hint of smoldering desires, and often you're not even aware of how much sensuality you exude. At other times, you deliberately turn on the waves of heat that shimmer around you. Unquestionably, you have powerful allure.

However, as with everything else in Scorpio's life, love and sex are complicated. Your character flaws show up more in romantic life than in other areas, and nothing brings out the extremes to which your nature is subject as much as sex.

To begin with, you make it difficult for someone to form a true, genuine relationship with you—not because you don't want a relationship. In fact, this is exactly what you want. You're an intensely sensitive person who often feels lonely and unfulfilled; your deepest desire is for a close, committed union. The problem is that jealousies and unexpressed angers are very difficult to live with. You have the most indefensible defenses in the zodiac. Although you can be easily hurt, you never let another see your vulnerable side—and you put up all your might against allowing anyone to dominate you.

Yet because you're attracted to powerful people, you set the stage for competition and control struggles. In addition, deep beneath your surface, menacing insecurities lurk, and you exercise strong restraints to keep these tamped down. The result is you're not only possessive and passionate, but secretly fearful and angry.

Also, something in you is galvanized by fatal sexual attractions. Scorpio represents things hidden, and you can easily become obsessed by an attraction that has intrigue and danger attached—for example, an affair that has to be secret, or a passion for someone with damaging psychological issues. You may gravitate to a lover who's unavailable emotionally and become fixated on making that person yours. You have an instinct for choosing relationships that quickly become problematical.

Nor are you interested in casual liaisons. Your reputation for possessiveness is well deserved, and anyone who thinks it isn't necessary to sign a treaty just because he or she is having an affair with you would do well to avoid getting involved with you. You believe in treaties with irrevocable clauses and lots of fine print spelling out just what your lover can't do.

If you're a Scorpio woman, you have a deeply sexual nature, but you do want to be courted and pursued. You can be the aggressor, but always in the most subtle and magnetic way. When you meet someone special, your dynamo starts to whir and you turn on your sensuality. If he's worthy of you, he won't have a faint heart. Once you're in a relationship, you cannot bear coldness or casualness or the feeling you're being shunted aside. You are very emotional, very affectionate, and very demanding. You're a fascinating woman—exciting in the bedroom, entertaining in the living room. You can drive a man to the brink of despair and with a gesture summon him back to the heights of happiness.

If you're a Scorpio male, you're aware of how attractive you are to women and make the most of it. In your approach, you plan your moves carefully, not wasting time but never appearing to be in haste. You're vigorous, virile, direct, and forceful. There aren't too many women around who can avoid responding to your uncomplicated physicality. One of the things that makes you unique as a lover is you truly understand a woman's needs and, if you're not threatened, will try to meet them.

Scorpio actually is less interested in sex per se than in *passion*. You want to be transported into another realm of feeling—and with the right partner, the sex between you can indeed be a spiritual uniting. You're gifted with the ability to penetrate into the secrets of human nature and therefore can see into a lover's sex fantasies. With your intense physical passion, you bring out the full sensual potential in anyone with whom you're having an intimate relationship.

When the thunderbolt hits and you do fall in love, your loyalty is legendary. The Scorpio in love is practically an archetype. What you demand is constancy, and what you offer is fidelity. Yours is a Fixed sign, and you commit yourself to nurturing, helping, and cherishing your lover. Whatever the cost, you will stand by the one you love; no one could have a fiercer ally. You will defend and protect with your dying breath, and merge yourself with this person you trust.

But should you ever lose that trust, there is no repairing it. A betrayal in love is a kind of death for you. Someone born under another sign might forgive and forget, but you will seethe and brood, wait for revenge, and always strike back. If necessary, you will destroy. And once the iron door has shut down, you will never turn back.

TIPS FOR THOSE WHO WANT TO ATTRACT SCORPIO

Scorpios are noted for their unpredictability, but here are a few general rules that may serve as a guide.

Listen to a Scorpio carefully with full attention. There's no way of faking it. Scorpios always know when you're pretending, and that will be the end before there's even a beginning.

Remember an overriding Scorpio trait: curiosity. Never tell a Scorpio that something happened without including the how or why. If you leave that out, you'll be classified as either dull or superficial. Neither type gets far with persons born under this sign.

Scorpios take an interest in New Age subjects, and discussions about UFOs, reincarnation, and psychic ability are sure to be lively.

They enjoy most forms of recreation, particularly water sports. If you're the type who likes a day at the beach or being out on a fishing boat or taking a waterskiing lesson, you and Scorpio will have that much in common. Scorpios also enjoy parties, social affairs, charity bazaars, and places where they can associate with successful people.

If you get into an argument (and you shouldn't with anyone born under this sign), please remember to be respectful. Scorpios are proud, serious, and don't believe that any of their opinions should be trifled with, even good-humoredly.

SCORPIO'S EROGENOUS ZONES:
Tips for Those with a Scorpio Lover

Our bodies are very sensitive to the touch of another human being. The special language of touching is understood on a level more basic than speech. Each sign is linked to certain zones and areas of the body that are especially receptive and can receive sexual message through touch. Many books and manuals have been written about lovemaking, but few pay attention to the unique knowledge of erogenous zones supplied by astrology. You can use astrology to become a better, more sensitive lover.

The genitals are everyone's erogenous zone, but for Scorpio the genitals are where sexual energy is exclusively focused and concentrated. Scorpio starts off with intense sexual feelings, and genital contact adds fuel to the fire. Even a light fingering of Scorpio's genital area will turn him or her into a volcano of passion.

There is almost no wrong way to touch and fondle Scorpio's genitals, unless you are inflicting pain. The following technique of erotic touching is a one good way to begin sexual arousal: Using fingertips or fingernails, stroke very lightly starting at one knee, up one thigh, across the genitals, and down the other thigh to just short of the other knee. Repeat in the opposite direction, but this time shorten the stroke by a few inches. Continue making each stroke shorter and shorter until you are just inches away from the genitals.

Since much of the excitement in erotic touching comes from anticipation, any manual or oral stimulation of the genitals should be done very slowly, and you should not always follow through as expected. "Teasing" with your fingertips can spur Scorpio on to the sexual heights.

SCORPIO'S AMOROUS COMBINATIONS: YOUR LOVE PARTNERS

SCORPIO AND ARIES

Your initial attraction is strong, for you're both highly sexual creatures. Aries can be a bit more imaginative and willing to experiment than you, but your smoldering eroticism proves a fair match. However, trouble looms in other areas. Both of you are selfish, and both want to make the decisions. There's a basic clash of wills because Aries wants to dominate and you want to control. Scorpio's secretiveness frustrates open, impulsive Aries. When you're angry, you tend to pull into yourself and brood, whereas Aries's conflict style is in-your-face. Aries is also freedom-loving, outgoing, and flirtatious—but your loving is possessive, and Aries easily triggers your jealousy. Temperamental differences shortly undermine your sexual rapport. A basic problem is Scorpio has emotional depth that Aries lacks, a fundamental inequity in your relationship that's very hard to bridge.

SCORPIO AND TAURUS

You're a pair of zodiacal opposites who are alike in many ways. You're strong, committed, and purposeful, and you share a high level of sensuality. Indeed, the sexual arena is where you two play most harmoniously, for Taurus has the stamina and desire to satisfy you in the bedroom. The question, though, is what are you two passionate people going to do with the other twenty-three and a half hours in the day. Both of you are very jealous and stubborn—the difference is that Taurus wants to own a lover like a valuable object, and you try to possess in an emotional sense. Though you share an affinity for finances, Scorpio tends to be thrifty and spurn laziness, whereas Taurus likes to spend on creature comforts. The Scorpio nature is willful, Taurus is obstinate, and unfortunately neither of you is likely to back down. You both want to be captain of what may turn out to be a sinking ship.

SCORPIO AND GEMINI

You're drawn to Gemini's vivacity and high spirits. In turn, curious Gemini is fascinated by your complex personality. Gemini is also greatly intrigued by your hypnotic sexuality—you light Gemini's erotic imagination. But what each of you needs from a relationship is very different because, essentially, Scorpio is an emotional sign and Gemini is cerebral. You want a psychic bonding, whereas Gemini looks for mental compatibility. You're intense and demand total commitment, and Gemini is far too changeable and inconstant for you. Restless Gemini has a strong penchant for independence, while you want to dominate and possess. You're both manipulative, but Scorpio will push dark emotional buttons and Gemini plays tricky mind games. Scorpio is basically a loner; Gemini likes to glitter in social settings. You'll have some lively frolics, but all too soon the fun palls—and Gemini starts looking for an exit.

SCORPIO AND CANCER

This can be a rewarding combination. Cancer is the passive partner, but there's plenty of combustible material to catch fire from Scorpio's abundant passions. Together, your lovemaking is mutually intense and deeply felt. The heat in the bedroom will help cool off disputes that can arise between two jealous people. You're both emotionally sensitive creatures with inborn radar for anything that threatens security—so you'll need to be careful about each other's vulnerabilities. However, strong Scorpio offers strength and protectiveness, which is just what clinging, insecure Cancer is looking for. In turn, Cancer is affectionate, generous, loving, and devoted—all that you want. Also, you both share a fondness for money, and each has creativity to pour into successful careers. You two get along together like bread and jam.

SCORPIO AND LEO

You're two proud, ambitious, determined people who have a hard time getting along. Passions and tempers are equally strong on both sides. To begin with, Scorpio is intense and darkly secretive, whereas Leo is all surface brightness who demands constant attention—but you won't flatter Leo's huge ego or accept Leo's dominance. In a love affair, you seek to plumb the erotic psyche of a lover, whereas Leo looks for a grand romance. Fiery Leo is extravagant and likes to live on a majestic scale, but you disapprove of conspicuousness and waste. There *is* extraordinary physical attraction between you two. Leo is an exuberant, over-the-top lover, and your Scorpio sexuality is profound, so lovemaking itself is not the problem. It's that you both are on a very short fuse. Your Scorpio jealousy will probably provide the spark, and when the explosion comes, the sky's the limit!

SCORPIO AND VIRGO

Restrained Virgo has trouble keeping up with highly demonstrative Scorpio and doesn't understand what all the fuss and bother is about. Yet Virgo can also be warm and earthy, especially because you're able to tap into Virgo's secret sex fantasies. Basically, you two have a marvelous meeting of minds and a fine mixing of personalities. Virgo will provide good emotional grounding for you and help smooth out practical problems. Virgo is levelheaded, likes to be of use, and fits in well as another pair of hands and eyes. Both of you are devoted to family and to financial security. Neither is flighty or superficial, and Virgo's faithfulness keeps your jealousy in check. Indeed, the deep feelings each of you harbors lead to a strong commitment and loyalty. You two have so much in common that maybe you won't mind that Virgo's passions are more intellectual than physical.

SCORPIO AND LIBRA

Your unpredictable nature immediately intrigues Libra, who enjoys collecting interesting people. You also satisfy Libra's need for attention—and then some—and your jealousy will flatter Libra. But Libra is an inconstant flirt, and you are supersensitive and touchy. Scorpio takes love and commitment seriously; Libra wants a partner to enhance its own image. Libra's on-again-off-again attitude toward love will frustrate and upset you. Libra lives on a more superficial level than you. Libra likes sweet pleasantries, a happy social life, and a harmonious environment—and avoids conflict like poison. You're at home with turbulent feelings and are very demanding emotionally. You definitely want a relationship that's intense and passionate. Also, Libra will try to escape from your possessive net. This mating isn't going to lead to anything permanent.

SCORPIO AND SCORPIO

You do have a chance of becoming soulmates who understand each other's desires and are willing to meld into the deep undercurrents of emotion. Certainly you share plenty of sexual attraction and will go with each other to the wilder shores of passion. But the emotional temperature can't keep rising forever. You two, who are so much alike, understand each other very little. The major hurdle in your pairing is that all the Scorpio negatives are doubled and the positives have no room to expand. You both are highly jealous and demanding. You're so intense that every little storm quickly becomes a hurricane. Both of you are sulky, brooding, possessive. Neither of you lets go or forgives, and both are in a continual struggle to force the other to relinquish control. Something has got to give. When it does, it's likely to spell the end.

SCORPIO AND SAGITTARIUS

You are tantalized by Sagittarius's freewheeling, risk-taking style. Especially, you're turned on by Sagittarius's uninhibited approach to sex. Lovemaking is dramatic and tempestuous—your deep, dark passions bring Sagittarius to the brink of ecstasy, and Sagittarius will give you anything you want sexually. However, your *personalities* will never mesh. Basically, Sagittarius doesn't want to deal with feelings, which is what you're all about. You will try to dominate, but Sagittarius flies off at the first hint of possessiveness. Sagittarius thinks the accent should be on fun and new adventure; you want security and constant loving. Sagittarius is open, talkative, and casual about relationships, whereas you are reticent, secretive, and very jealous in love. You want Sagittarius at home; Sagittarius wants to roam. An affair without a future.

SCORPIO AND CAPRICORN

All of your powerful passions find a welcome here. Separately, each of you can be unapproachable, but together you create a rich and passionate coupling. Your volatile emotions open up brooding, inner-directed Capricorn—with you, Capricorn delights in newfound pleasures of the flesh. Your zesty sexual goings-on add savor to a warm emotional relationship. Capricorn is not as intuitive as you, but your intense commitment brings out Capricorn's deep loyalty. Capricorn even likes your jealousy, for this makes Capricorn feel secure. In turn, Capricorn's devotion to work and a good lifestyle provides you with solid grounding. You two share a sense of purpose—each of you is ambitious, determined, and serious about responsibility, and as a team you have good auguries for financial success. Together you have clear sailing.

SCORPIO AND AQUARIUS

Astrologically, you come from different planets. You're the flesh-and-blood human being who wants to live life. Aquarius operates from a brilliant computer-brain that wants to think about life. You feel intensely and crave intimacy; Aquarius has a distant quality and mainly wants friendship. Sex is fine technically speaking, but you can't get from Aquarius the deep, raw passion you need. To Aquarius, even a love affair is simply another way to broaden its horizons—and Aquarius is altogether too impersonal and has too many outside interests to suit you. You find it painful to put up with Aquarius's casual air toward love. You want to dominate and possess, and will never understand Aquarius's independence. You're upset by Aquarius's unpredictable moods. You want to stay at home; Aquarius wants to be free to go. And so on—to the finish.

SCORPIO AND PISCES

Both of you are intuitive, emotional Water signs who thrive together. Even the ways in which you're not alike work. You're fixed and stubborn, but Pisces, being flexible and adaptable, can flow into what you demand. Certainly, your Scorpio strength is a perfect bulwark for Pisces's indecisiveness. In turn, Pisces's imagination sparks your creativity. Pisces is able to give you the devotion and admiration you crave, and your mutual fascination with lovemaking provides a fine romantic aura. Sexually, Pisces is highly expressive and has an appetite that beautifully matches your Scorpio eroticism. Indeed, Pisces's flair for the bizarre adds spice to your desires, and the intense emotional needs of both your signs neatly complement each other. Pisces's intuitive awareness and your Scorpio depth of feeling unite in a special closeness. This kind of mating lasts.

YOUR SCORPIO CAREER PATH

Power and control, the Scorpio themes that are so much a part of your character, infuse your professional life. Success is all-important, the *sine qua non*—but the Scorpio definition of success is likely to be different from what it means to others. Your psychic drive (sometimes unconscious) is to transform. Whatever you take hold of has to be something you can mold and direct and make into an entity changed from its beginnings. You're a creator and director who constructs what was not there to start with. Often you're the power behind the throne, for you're the one who pulls the strings.

Thus, you're at your best being in charge, working at your own pace (usually high-speed), and answering to no one. Of course, this optimum situation is uncommon, generally not feasible or available—yet elements of this must be present in your work for you to feel successful (in Scorpio's definition).

You enjoy uncovering the inner workings of an enterprise—the underlying concepts and how a project is put together. Your way of thinking is to separate the components and rearrange them differently. You figure out what will make the venture better, what it needs to be more productive or appealing, and you instinctively know how to set change into motion. Equally comfortable in the business sphere and the artistic world, you bring precision to creative projects and an imaginative approach to finance and merchandising.

You're a quick learner and quickly gravitate toward positions of trust and responsibility. Even if you begin on the lowest rung you speedily ascend. You're shrewd, organized, meticulous; you possess a probing mind, a steel-trap memory, and ferocious tenacity. When you set your mind to solving a problem, you solve a problem. Others stand in awe of your computer brain and talent for digging out facts. You're also marvelous at galvanizing the talents of those around you to get what you want done. Your strength may be sheathed in a velvet glove, but there's no question you're a leader.

The quality that truly puts you in a separate class is your strong-willed patience. Your undeviating pursuit of a goal is one of your strongest assets. You're a rare being who can achieve anything your heart truly desires. Indeed, you have every attribute needed for success because you combine a warrior's courage with the power to drive through obstacles. The only thing that can hold you back is you yourself, in particular your fear of success.

You may not acknowledge this fear, but it lurks in your secret depths—and your Scorpio career path is a journey to overcome your fears and learn to be comfortable with your fierce inborn power.

As has been said, you live on many levels, and within your complex makeup is a deep sense of purpose. You need work that has importance and touches other people. You do this with your art, products you sell, finances you handle, your writing, teaching, administrating, investigating. Whatever you put yourself into makes an impact.

Your talent for research may lead you toward work in science, mathematics, astronomy, archeology, and computer technology. You're also drawn to the healing professions, such as social work or medicine; you'd make a good surgeon, psychiatrist, or therapist. In the financial arena, your skills can qualify you as an investor, banker or accountant. You're a consummate actor (who conceals an intense private life) and you can put this skill into work as a performing artist. You have a talent for acting, dance, music, painting, and photography.

Work is among your most vital expressions, and it does devour a great deal of your essential force. You pour your passion into achieving an objective, and once you've reached a pinnacle, you keep moving upward on an ascending scale. Your issues therefore are twofold. You can burn yourself out with the striving, and your steam engine can consume you. You need to learn to balance work with other aspects of your life—relationships, family, social interaction, recreation, hobbies.

The second challenge is how to cope when you are thwarted and impeded. When any kind of flow in your life is blocked, it can do serious internal damage. It can deaden your feelings and certainly stand in the way of your caring about others. It can paralyze you as you mark time, make excuses, stuff down your rage and fears, and become ever more arrogant and a braggadocio. Eventually, it can manifest in physical illness.

The only way to counteract this is to learn how not to be controlled by your need to control, to learn how to flow. Scorpio is a Water sign and a Fixed sign, but if you keep that Fixed Water moving, you're capable of great fluidity. Instead of damming up feelings and retreating further into yourself, you can move through perceived failure. No one is more able to start on another track and continue creating. You're the sign of endings and new beginnings, the one who can rise from the ashes and become even more powerful. You're like the tides, and utilizing your power of ebb and flow is intrinsic to your success in a career.

SCORPIO AND HEALTH: ADVICE FROM ASTROLOGY

Your health is inextricably tied to your intense emotional makeup. For you, stress triggers bodily dysfunction and disease. You tend to dam up feelings (such as anger, anxiety, worry) and the only outlet for this turbulence to pour into is your body. You're also a compulsive worker and, though you have vast reserves of energy, you can deplete them. In addition when your mind becomes overcharged, you suffer from insomnia. Happily, Scorpio is the sign of regeneration, and with minimum care you can restore and rejuvenate. Healthy food will fuel you, and a modicum of exercise will dissipate tension. Certainly, you need demanding challenges in your life, for you'd otherwise sink into discontent. Yet your health lesson is to establish balance between work, relationships, and recreation—and especially to be aware of what demons (drink, drugs, etc.) will take you over the edge.

Advice and useful tips about health are among the most important kinds of information that astrology provides. Health and well-being are of paramount concern to human beings. Love, money, or career takes second place, for without good health we cannot enjoy anything in life.

Astrology and medicine have had a long marriage. Hippocrates (born around 460 B.C.), the Greek philosopher and physician who is considered the father of medicine, said, "A physician without a knowledge of astrology has no right to call himself a physician." Indeed, up until the eighteenth century, the study of astrology and its relationship to the body was very much a part of a doctor's training. When a patient became ill, a chart was immediately drawn up. This guided the doctor in both diagnosis and treatment, for the chart would tell when the crisis would come and what medicine would help. Of course, modern Western doctors no longer use astrology to treat illness. However, astrology can still be a useful tool in helping to understand and maintain our physical well-being.

THE PART OF THE BODY RULED BY SCORPIO

Each sign of the zodiac governs a specific part of the body. These associations date back to the beginning of astrology. Curiously, the part of the body that a sign rules is in some ways the strongest and in other ways the weakest area for natives of that sign.

Your sign of Scorpio rules the sexual organs. Symbolically, this part of the anatomy represents life-giving force, and Scorpios are renowned for their fund of energy and imagination. You have a reputation for being highly sexed, passionate, and possessive, someone who does nothing halfway. A healthy sex life is essential to your well-being. Scorpio even takes out anger in sexual ways: you use or withhold sex as a weapon. Sexual frustration or suppression of intense feelings results in erratic and cruel behavior in many Scorpios.

As a native of Scorpio, you're prone to problems and infections of the sex organs. Skin eruptions on the genitals, cystitis and diseases of the urinary tract, and venereal infections are ailments to which Scorpios are most susceptible.

In addition, you're subject to ill health brought on by emotional issues. Your intense nature tends to brood and seethe over insults and injuries (often imagined). You seem unable to rest and relax, and as a result may suffer from exhaustion.

Your sign of Scorpio is ruled by the planet Pluto, which governs the formation of cells and the reproductive function of the body. Thus, Scorpio's link with sex and regenerative forces is strengthened. As a rule, you have a strong, voluptuous body and excellent recuperative powers—though some astrologers have remarked on the fact that more people born under Scorpio come to a violent and unexpected end than do natives of other signs. Do not be alarmed by this; simply take it as a caution to look after yourself and not let your deep desires lead you astray. It's been said that Scorpios look old when they are young, and young when they are old.

DIET AND HEALTH TIPS FOR SCORPIO

A healthful diet is important in order to keep up your energy and a positive outlook on life. When problems strike, you have a tendency to overindulge in alcohol and forget about food, which in turn makes you more unhappy, listless, and ill.

Scorpio has a problem handling liquor. Of all the signs in the zodiac, alcohol has the worst and most immediate effects on your looks and skin. It is toxic for your system, it intensifies your already volatile emotions, and most Scorpios don't know how to say no to a second drink.

Scorpio's cell salt* is calcium sulphate, which is the prime factor in the repair of tissues and resistance to infectious diseases. The nose, mouth, throat, esophagus, reproductive organs, and intestinal pathways need this mineral for healthy functioning. A deficiency opens the way to colds and sinus infections that hang on forever, skin eruptions that do not heal, and infertility. Foods rich in calcium sulphate that you should include in your diet are asparagus, kale, cauliflower, radishes, onions, parsnips, watercress, tomatoes, figs, prunes, black cherries, and coconuts. You need calcium foods such as milk, cheese, yogurt, and cottage cheese. You should concentrate on a diet high in protein, fresh fruits and vegetables, and whole-grain breads.

The following are particularly good for you: fish and seafood, green salads, beets, escarole, romaine, brussels sprouts, artichokes, lentils, wheat germ, almonds, walnuts, citrus fruit, berries, apples, bananas, and pineapples. You should not eat large meals, and the evening meal should be light. Bottled spring water is often better for you to drink than regular tap water.

In general, you need rest and recreation, exercise, and peaceful surroundings. Born under a Water sign, you benefit from sea travel, vacations at the seashore, and long soaks in warm baths.

*Cell salts (also known as tissue salts) are mineral compounds found in human tissue cells. These minerals are the only substances our cells cannot produce by themselves. The life of cells is relatively short, and the creation of new cells depends on the presence of these minerals.

THE DECANATES AND CUSPS OF SCORPIO

Decanate and *cusp* are astrological terms that subdivide your Sun sign. These subdivisions further define and emphasize certain qualities and character traits of your Sun sign Scorpio.

WHAT IS A DECANATE?

Each astrological sign is divided into three parts, and each part is called a *decanate* or a *decan* (the terms are used interchangeably).

The word comes from the Greek word *dekanoi*, meaning "ten days apart." The Greeks took their word from the Egyptians, who divided their year into 360 days.* The Egyptian year had twelve months of thirty days each, and each month was further divided into three sections of ten days each. It was these ten-day sections the Greeks called *dekanoi*.

*The Egyptians soon found out that a 360-day year was inaccurate and so added on five extra days. These were feast days and holidays, and not counted as real days.

Astrology still divides the zodiac into decanates. There are twelve signs in the zodiac, and each sign is divided into three decanates. You might picture each decanate as a room. You were born in the sign of Scorpio, which consists of three rooms (decanates). In which room of Scorpio were you born?

The zodiac is a 360-degree circle. Each decanate is ten degrees of that circle, or about ten days long, since the Sun moves through the zodiac at approximately the rate of one degree per day. (This is not exact because not all of our months contain thirty days.)

The decanate of a sign does not change the basic characteristics of that sign, but it does refine and individualize the sign's general characteristics. If you were born, say, in the second decanate of Scorpio, it does not change the fact you are a Scorpio. It does indicate that you have somewhat different and special characteristics from those Scorpio people born in the first decanate or the third decanate.

Finally, each decanate has a specific planetary ruler, sometimes called a subruler because it does not usurp the overall rulership of your sign. The subruler can only enhance and add to the distinct characteristics of your decanate. For example, your entire sign of Scorpio is ruled by Pluto, but the second decanate of Scorpio is subruled by Neptune. The influence of Neptune, the subruler, combines with the overall authority of Pluto to make the second decanate of Scorpio unlike any other in the zodiac.

FIRST DECANATE OF SCORPIO

October 23 through November 1
Keyword: Integrity
Constellation: Serpens, the Serpent, symbolizing power and occult knowledge.
Planetary Subruler: Pluto

Pluto is both your ruler and subruler, which gives a hypnotic intensity to your personality. You are loyal and steadfast, and others quickly sense they can depend on you. You will stand by a lover long after others in the same situation would let go. Once you let go, however, there is usually no turning back. You have fixed opinions, but also a scientific turn of mind that will examine ideas and arrive at a new opinion should the facts warrant it. You are drawn to the mysterious and the occult but may keep this a secret. Should you choose to use it, you have great power of self-discipline. Sometimes you let things slide by because you don't care enough to exert yourself.

SECOND DECANATE OF SCORPIO

November 2 through November 11
Keyword: Regeneration
Constellation: Lupus, the Wolf, held aloft by Centaurus. The Wolf symbolizes offering.
Planetary Subruler: Neptune

Neptune, planet of sensitivity, combines with Scorpio's Pluto to accentuate an idealistic personality. In both work and love, you tend to reach out toward others and give of yourself. You would make a superb teacher, healer, or physician; you have a talent for inspiring and helping others. It is important to you to find deeper meaning in your relationships. You are romantic and intense, and love fulfills and completes you. Once you can find contentment in love, you reach your true potential in other areas of life. Generally, your luck comes through other people when you least expect it. You are not a patient person and find it difficult to wait for the slow unfolding of events in your life.

THIRD DECANATE OF SCORPIO

November 12 through November 21
Keyword: Clarification
Constellation: Aquila, the Eagle, whom the Greeks considered the only creature able to outstare the Sun. The Eagle is symbolic of rising above earthly limitations.
Planetary Subruler: Moon

The sensuous Moon combines with Scorpio's Pluto to give an allure to your personality. You are at your best dealing with groups of people, and tend to choose work that projects you into the public eye. Your magnetic social touch wins popularity. Fate seems to thrust you into situations or relationships that you do not pick, but are often the most successful for you. You have a strong sense of ethics, and injustice brings out your fighting spirit. At times you can be moody, especially when the actions of other people discourage you. You have deep emotions that you have difficulty sharing. Once you reveal yourself, you are direct and honest and don't evade the truth.

A cusp is the point at which a new astrological sign begins.* Thus, the cusp of Scorpio means the point at which Scorpio begins. (The word comes from the Latin word *cuspis*, meaning "point.")

When someone speaks of being "born on the cusp," that person is referring to a birth time at or near the beginning or the end of an astrological sign. For example, if you were born on November 21, you were born on the cusp of Sagittarius, the sign that begins on November 22. Indeed, depending on what year you were born, your birth time might even be in the first degree of Sagittarius. People born on the very day a sign begins or ends are often confused about what sign they really are—a confusion made more complicated by the fact that the Sun does not move into or out of a sign at *exactly* the same moment (or even day) each year. There are slight time differences from year to year. Therefore, if you are a Scorpio born on October 23 or November 21, you'll find great clarity consulting a computer chart that tells you exactly where the Sun was at the very moment you were born.

As for what span of time constitutes being born on the cusp, the astrological community holds various opinions. Some astrologers claim cusp means being born only within the first two days or last two days of a sign (though many say this is too narrow a time frame). Others say it can be as much as within the first ten days or last ten days of a sign (which many say is too wide an interpretation). The consensus is that you were born on the cusp if your birthday is within the first *five* days or last *five* days of a sign.

*In a birth chart, a cusp is also the point at which an astrological House begins.

The question hanging over cusp-born people is "What sign am I really?" They feel they straddle the border of two different countries. To some extent, this is true. If you were born on the cusp, you're under the influence of both signs. However, much like being a traveler leaving one country and crossing into another, you must actually *be* in one country—you can't be in two countries at the same time. One sign is always a stronger influence, and that sign is almost invariably the sign that the Sun was actually in (in other words, your Sun sign). The reason I say "almost" is that in rare cases a chart may be so heavily weighted with planets in a certain sign that the person more keenly feels the influence of that specific sign.

For example, I have a client who was born in the evening on November 21. On that evening, the Sun was leaving Scorpio and entering Sagittarius. At the moment of her birth, the Sun was still in Scorpio, so technically speaking she is a Scorpio. However, the Sun was only a couple hours away from being in Sagittarius, and this person has the Moon, Mercury, and Venus all in Sagittarius. She has always felt like a Sagittarian and always behaved as a Sagittarian.

This, obviously, is an unusual case. Generally, the Sun is the most powerful planetary influence in a chart. Even if you were born with the Sun on the very tip of the first or last degree of Scorpio, Scorpio is your Sun sign—and this is the sign you will most feel like.

Still, the influence of the approaching sign or of the sign just ending is present, and you will probably sense that mixture in yourself.

BORN OCTOBER 23 THROUGH OCTOBER 27

You are Scorpio with Libra tendencies. There is an elegance to your personality, a charm and good-naturedness that people respond to. You have a talent for expressing your opinions in an apt and amusing way. You have a strong will, but unless you are crossed or thwarted, you don't often show it. In general, you are cooperative and friendly, even though you prefer to work alone at your own pace. This is especially true in any creative enterprise. In love, your feelings run deep, and you tend to be cautious. You don't commit yourself easily because you fear being hurt or rejected.

BORN NOVEMBER 17 THROUGH NOVEMBER 21

You are Scorpio with Sagittarius tendencies. You are sensitive, intuitive, and likely have a lot of nervous energy. You enjoy a variety of interests and hobbies and attract different types of friends. Mental activity stimulates you. You are fond of discussion and are never reluctant to share an opinion. Those you love are aware of your loyalty and warm feelings; others usually see you as someone who makes dispassionate judgments. The truth is that you are sentimental, but you are able to stand back and be objective if this is in your best interests. You do have a strong romantic streak.

YOUR SPECIAL DAY OF BIRTH

OCTOBER 23

You are generous, passionate, and perhaps too trusting—your romantic heart leads you into unusual byways. You have poetic imagination. In a career, your great strengths are your powers of observation and a charming sense of humor.

OCTOBER 24

In work, you produce results because you have fixed concentration. Emotionally, though, you are full of ebb and flow. You pick up currents of feelings from others, and lovers find you deeply sensitive and sexual. Be careful about becoming overly possessive.

OCTOBER 25

You're open, friendly, and talkative, and people call you a character. Yet your outer personality is quite different from your inner life, which is deep and spiritual. You're very loving—the problem is you get caught up in what others want and put yourself last.

OCTOBER 26

Following orders is not your thing—you have the brave assurance to stand up for your own opinions. Yet no one could be more loyal and accommodating. In love, especially, you're a wholehearted, passionate giver with abundant sensuality.

OCTOBER 27

Creativity runs in your veins, though you have a hard time channeling your imagination. You're also intensely charismatic in matters of love and sex. Romantic attachments are tumultuous, but ultimately you're promised happiness with a soulmate.

OCTOBER 28

You have a warm, radiant personality and appear completely confident. Actually, though, you're always aware of others' responses toward you and adjust accordingly. You're risk averse, and yet in love you'll jump the chasm without a moment's hesitation.

OCTOBER 29

You're tough but tender. Relationships are central, yet you can be off-putting to those who care for you most. In your work, you have a creative, think-out-of-the-box approach—and when you lose your heart in love, you're consumed with raw passion.

OCTOBER 30

The impression you give of being scattered is really your super-intelligent brain whirring away with ideas. You're highly sociable, very idealistic, and quite ambitious. You can be flirtatious, but when you fall in love, you're extremely loyal.

OCTOBER 31

Animated and communicative, you have strong ethics and are very honest. Mental inquisitiveness leads you into unusual career paths until you find the perfect fit. In love, your emotions are deep, but you tend to make choices for sacrificial reasons.

NOVEMBER 1

People are drawn to your great warmth and intelligence, and few know that secretly you're shy. You're caring, honest, and true to your word, and you make friends for life. You're just as loyal in love but must learn to choose someone worthy of you.

NOVEMBER 2

You're tuned to your own inner voice, and in work and lifestyle are original and daring. Paradoxically, you're also very sensitive and can be easily hurt. In love, you tend to complicate your life by holding on too long and refusing to look at reality.

NOVEMBER 3

Restless and impatient, you're taken for a rebel though actually you just need space to do your thing without interference. Your true rebel heart shows up in romance, for you'll give your all to someone you love no matter what advice you get from others.

NOVEMBER 4

You're a people person, although you tend to mother others and attract the overly needy. In work, you're a perfectionist. Love can be complicated because your sensuality entices those you're not interested in. But when the thunderbolt strikes, you're fervent.

NOVEMBER 5

Basically, you can't get both your head and heart together. On one side passions drive you; on the other duty calls. You're unusual and talented—and in time you'll pour all your intensity into perfect work and profound love.

NOVEMBER 6

You live in your intense feelings yet are airily at ease in the public. Your powerful tool is your brilliant mind—you're able to dissect problems and people, and find answers. In love, you're sexual *and* romantic. You need grand passion but are often disappointed.

NOVEMBER 7

A wide variety of people responds to your magnetism. You bring cheer and lightheartedness. Yet you, yourself, feel weighed down by heavy responsibility—and unwarranted guilt. Inwardly, you're a creature of romantic fantasy you find hard to fulfill in real life.

NOVEMBER 8

You have a fragile heart, but the rest of you is very strong. You possess logic and imagination in equal measure, and in your work, you are known as a powerhouse who can get things done. Only a special lover can fit your whims, needs, desires, and lusts.

NOVEMBER 9

You have a radiant lovability many Scorpios do not have, and people crowd around you. In work, your specialty is to translate feelings into creative ideas. In love, you need passion and emotional security—take extra care that your lover is worthy of you.

NOVEMBER 10

Whatever you go through (and you've gone through a lot) keeps leading you to a special destiny that takes you far from your beginnings. In love, you long for depth and magic. After trial and error, you'll be in a relationship that lasts forever.

NOVEMBER 11

Victory is your middle name—your dramatic life has taught you that you were born to be different and blaze your own trail. Your eye for quality and detail put you in a rarified class. You're talented, passionate, and have an earthy sensuality and a poetic, romantic streak.

NOVEMBER 12

Some think you're eccentric, and all see you as decisive—and lucky. Indeed, you attract luck because you make choices from your heart and follow your own rules. Sexually, you're very tempting to others, but you have high standards and only the crème de la crème appeals.

NOVEMBER 13

You're highly motivated and a bit vain (though you deserve to be), and what you want is never what others tell you is the right path.

You're an explorer who can also build firm foundations. Sexually, your world is often chaotic, and it will be until you find your own true self.

NOVEMBER 14

Living the good life is important, and for you this does not only mean having money. You want adventure and to be an achiever. You have a theatrical sense of the beauty and tragedy of life. Your charismatic personality tends to turn your love affairs into competitive affairs.

NOVEMBER 15

There's a long-distance runner in you—you go the distance. Your perseverance attracts those looking for a strong center (especially in love)—but you need to be less sacrificing emotionally. Curiously, you're also independent, and some lovers complain you're aloof.

NOVEMBER 16

You think you're scattered and unable to get to everything on your to-do list. But your restless mind saves you from getting trapped in other people's agendas. Where you need to slow down and open up is in love relationships; you have a tendency to back away too soon.

NOVEMBER 17

You're a mold-breaker; whatever you put your hand to turns out unlike anything anyone has created before. You're an outsider because others can't see as far as you. Emotionally, you're deep, complicated, forceful, and passionate, yet also surprisingly shy.

NOVEMBER 18

You're an introvert in extrovert clothing, and you are greatly respected for being a good counselor to others. In your own life, you need to focus—you have trouble with distractions. To find perfect love is your journey, but you're promised a high-voltage romance that lasts.

NOVEMBER 19

You're fascinated by mystery, how people's minds work, how to solve problem; you're interested in spiritual questions and the occult. In any close relationship, communicating is essential. In love, you're cerebral yet also erotically sensual and deeply devoted.

NOVEMBER 20

Engaging, sincere, a dreamer, and a prodigious achiever when your interest is engaged, you find it hard to fit in "normal" society.

You're meant to translate your feelings into work with a lasting quality. In love, you can be deeply involved, but your roving eye can also complicate your life.

NOVEMBER 21

In matters of the heart, you don't have answers, but in everything else you do. You're vibrant, funny, loveable, a cagey thinker, and brilliant in your work. Love is problematical because you want to please and also to dominate. You're highly responsive sexually.

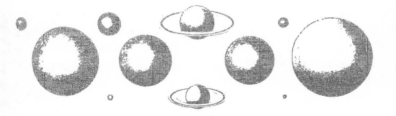

YOU AND CHINESE ASTROLOGY

With Marco Polo's adventurous travels in A.D. 1275, Europeans learned for the first time of the great beauty, wealth, history, and romance of China. Untouched as they were by outside influences, the Chinese developed their astrology along different lines from other ancient cultures, such as the Egyptians, Babylonians, and Greeks from whom Western astrology has its roots. Therefore, the Chinese zodiac differs from the zodiac of the West. To begin with, it is based on a lunar cycle rather than Western astrology's solar cycle. The Chinese zodiac is divided into twelve years, and each year is represented by a different animal—the rat, ox, tiger, rabbit, dragon, snake, horse, goat, monkey, rooster, dog, and pig. The legend of the twelve animals is that when Buddha lay on his deathbed, he asked the animals of the forest to come and bid him farewell. These twelve were the first to arrive. The cat, as the story goes, is not among the animals because it was napping and couldn't be bothered to make the journey. (In some Asian countries, however, such as Vietnam, the cat replaces the rabbit.)

Like Western astrology, in which the zodiac signs have different characteristics, each of the twelve Chinese animal years assigns character traits specific to a person born in that year. For example, the Year of the Rat confers honesty and an analytical mind, whereas the Year of the Monkey grants charm and quick ability to spot opportunity.

Here are descriptions for Scorpio for each Chinese animal year:

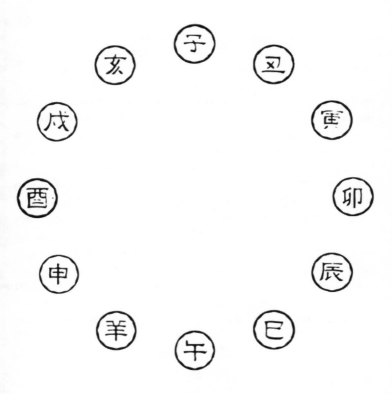

IF YOU ARE SCORPIO BORN IN THE YEAR OF THE RAT

Years of the Rat

1900	1960	2020	2080
1912	1972	2032	2092
1924	1984	2044	
1936	1996	2056	
1948	2008	2068	

In the West, rats are thought of as dirty and repugnant, but in Asia the Rat is a magnetic creature of charm, wit, high intelligence, seductiveness, and sociability. The Year of the Rat always ushers in renewal and speeded-up activity—and as a Rat native, you're said to be ambitious, resourceful, and inventive. Rat characteristics of charisma and an analytical mind magnify your Scorpio ability to move relentlessly toward a goal. One of your striking talents is a prescient sense of upcoming events and trends, so you're always a step ahead. You're also a meddler and complainer, but you get away with this because you're so appealing. The Scorpio Rat is not without guile—you look out for yourself and those you love. Indeed, in love you're overprotective and very passionate, and you do all in your power to keep a lover happy. Compatible partners are born in the Years of the Monkey, Pig, Rat, and Snake.

IF YOU ARE SCORPIO BORN IN THE YEAR OF THE OX

Years of the Ox

1901	1961	2021	2081
1913	1973	2033	2093
1925	1985	2045	
1937	1997	2057	
1949	2009	2069	

The Chinese Ox is eloquent and imaginative and powered by a great sense of purpose. Ox qualities of dedication and discipline blend beautifully with your Scorpio intensity—born in the Year of the Ox, you have double the willpower of other Scorpios. In addition, you have the personal magnetism to lead large groups of people, and are particularly successful in creative and intellectual fields. It's true you're domineering (how could you not be?) and never yield what you consider your territory. Basically, you search for stability but have an adventurous streak that will take you to far-flung places and unusual subjects. In love, you're deeply loyal, and when someone can truly touch your heart, you're a goner. At times you can be naively self-sacrificing, which causes you heartache. Compatible partners are born in the Years of the Rabbit, Rooster, Monkey, Pig, and Snake.

IF YOU ARE SCORPIO BORN IN THE YEAR OF THE TIGER

Years of the Tiger

1902	1962	2022	2082
1914	1974	2034	2094
1926	1986	2046	
1938	1998	2058	
1950	2010	2070	

The Tiger is filled with passion, intellectual courage, and super-audacity. Tiger zeal and spontaneity add to your Scorpio power of persuasion to give you arresting magnetism and an allure few can resist. Your dazzle fascinates people, and you always stand out in a crowd. One thing that sets you apart is you make daring life choices others would shrink from. As a Scorpio Tiger, you're a revolutionary who pours your dedication into off-the-beaten-track artistic work, and you work like a demon. Yet it is to relationships that you give your true life force. You need authentic and intense connections of the heart, and are a faithful friend. In love, your sensuality is exotic and erotic, but, sadly, most lovers cannot fill your deep desires. You also have a penchant for choosing lovers who need *you* more than you need them. Compatible partners are born in the Years of the Rabbit, Dog, Dragon, Monkey, Tiger, and Pig.

IF YOU ARE SCORPIO BORN IN THE YEAR OF THE RABBIT

Years of the Rabbit

1903	1963	2023	2083
1915	1975	2035	2095
1927	1987	2047	
1939	1999	2059	
1951	2011	2071	

The Asian Rabbit (or, in countries such as Vietnam, the Cat) is theatrical, talkative, and blessed with rich imagination and a strong creative bent. Born in the Year of the Rabbit, you always appear smart, savvy, and self-assured. Indeed, Rabbit poise and the ability to handle tricky situations add to your Scorpio cool. Your outward calm disguises a computer brain whirring away inside and a blazing ambition. Odd that some call you superficial and a dilettante, but this is because you care only about what lights your passions. In work, you're a natural performer who can mesmerize a crowd. In romantic affairs, you have a straying eye—but when love's thunderbolt strikes, you become intensely attached. Compatible partners are born in the Years of the Goat, Dog, Dragon, Snake, Horse, and Monkey.

IF YOU ARE SCORPIO BORN IN THE YEAR OF THE DRAGON

Years of the Dragon

1904	1964	2024	2084
1916	1976	2036	2096
1928	1988	2048	
1940	2000	2060	
1952	2012	2072	

The Chinese Dragon is immortal, a magnificent creature symbolizing the realization of dreams. The Dragon has heroism, perseverance, and poetic imagination. When Dragon qualities of exuberance, pride, idealism are added to your Scorpio willpower and intensity, the results are a powerhouse personality destined to step into an unusual role. You have great personal charm and a sense of extravagance. These are super tools for achieving success because your ambitions are grand, and you need the public to perceive you as larger than life. Your work is highly individualistic, though Scorpio Dragon usually has to go through an early "mini-failure" before finding what catapults you into stardom. Emotionally, you're a sentimental soft touch and an abundantly sexual being. In love, you're apt to be jealous, but also need a lot of freedom. Compatible partners are born in the Years of the Rabbit, Goat, Monkey, Snake, and Tiger.

IF YOU ARE SCORPIO BORN IN THE YEAR OF THE SNAKE

Years of the Snake

1905	1965	2025	2085
1917	1977	2037	2097
1929	1989	2049	
1941	2001	2061	
1953	2013	2073	

In the West, the snake connotes danger and evil temptation, but the Eastern Snake is aligned with the Goddess of Love. The Snake has beauty, creativity, and magical elegance. The Year of the Snake always brings new discovery, a theme that marks your adventurous life. Snake wisdom, intuition, confidence, and passion all combine with your Scorpio magnetism to create someone of extraordinary intelligence, fluency of speech, leadership skill, and a captivating personality. You also possess physical attractiveness—no small factor in your allure. You enjoy a life of luxury, are strongly creative, and have a more flamboyant stage presence than other Scorpios. As for romance, your sensual glow can literally enslave lovers. Yet you need something deeper, a soul-and-sexual connection that transports a love affair out of the ordinary. Compatible partners are born in the Years of the Rabbit, Rooster, Dragon, Horse, Ox, and Rat.

IF YOU ARE SCORPIO BORN IN THE YEAR OF THE HORSE

Years of the Horse

1906	1966	2026	2086
1918	1978	2038	2098
1930	1990	2050	
1942	2002	2062	
1954	2014	2074	

The Horse carries awesome power and is considered so significant that in Asia pregnancies are planned around the Year of the Horse. The Horse connotes sovereignty, magnificence, dedication, and inspiration. Its courage and commitment blend with your Scorpio tenacity, making you a crusader who can't conform to the ordinary. Scorpio Horse won't be held in check, and you're often described as a loose cannon. You have the heart of a daring adventurer. Yet you can be practical, applying your intellect to solving difficult problems—often in your work, where you have a genius for designing new products or strategies. In love, you're sought after by those who want to dominate you, and relationships become a power struggle. As you grow wiser, you'll connect body and soul to a person casual observers would never predict would interest you. Compatible partners are born in the Years of the Rabbit, Rooster, Goat, Horse, and Snake.

IF YOU ARE SCORPIO BORN IN THE YEAR OF THE GOAT

Years of the Goat

1907	1967	2027	2087
1919	1979	2039	2099
1931	1991	2051	
1943	2003	2063	
1955	2015	2075	

The Western goat has a humorous, often sexual connotation, but in China the Goat is intelligent and sensitive, and symbolizes artistic invention. The Goat's talent to create blends with Scorpio perseverance and practicality—endowing you with a gift for making money. You're a dreamer who's lucky; you have a propensity for flowing into the right channels. As a Scorpio Goat, you can climb high on the social scale, marry well, and enjoy lucrative work. True, you must be pushed, for you tend to wander off into paths that promise pleasure rather than hard work. You do best linked to someone (in love or business) who recognizes your unusual genius and keeps you on track. In romance, your charm and sweet sexuality are a great draw. But you have a dissatisfied heart and may have a number of unfulfilling affairs before you find lasting security in love. Compatible partners are born in the Years of the Rabbit, Dragon, Horse, Monkey, and Pig.

IF YOU ARE SCORPIO BORN IN THE YEAR OF THE MONKEY

Years of the Monkey

1908	1968	2028	2088
1920	1980	2040	2100
1932	1992	2052	
1944	2004	2064	
1956	2016	2076	

In Asian mythology, the Monkey is the amusing companion to the God of Sailors, bringing cheer on long voyages—and vivacity and wit are part of your personality. Also, a special Monkey trait is an ability to cover up feelings, and all these qualities blend with Scorpio introspection to make you an extroverted introvert. Scorpio Monkey is an actor with loquacious charm and a detective eye for seeing past the public faces others put on. You have a quick, agile mind and insatiable curiosity—as well as a built-in radar for spotting opportunity. People do say you're nosy and also devious, but usually when they're taken aback that you've uncovered their secrets. Emotionally, you're complicated—sensitive yet able to deflect slings and arrows. Only someone deep and brilliant can get to you. You're highly sexual, and lovers adore the eroticism you bring to an affair. Compatible partners are born in the Years of the Rabbit, Dragon, Ox, Pig, Rat, and Tiger.

IF YOU ARE SCORPIO BORN IN THE YEAR OF THE ROOSTER

Years of the Rooster

1909	1957	2005	2053
1921	1969	2017	2065
1933	1981	2029	2077
1945	1993	2041	2089

In Asia, the Rooster is dedicated to the Goddess of the Sun, whom he saved from danger—and symbolizes courage. The Rooster is sincere, enterprising, feisty, and loyal. Rooster brilliance and outspokenness meld with your Scorpio drive and clarity of expression. Thus, you're a resourceful and talented leader to whom others pay attention (even if you are a bit bossy and overbearing). You're grounded, yet you have high-flying ideas. Happily, your daring concepts produce results. You also have an instinct for making money, though it slips quickly through your fingers. True, your life is filled with ups and downs—but people enjoy your spirited energy, and you're extremely popular. You have a definite sex appeal, and it's easy to find someone to play with. But for long-term commitment, you choose carefully. You have a giving heart and don't want it to be broken. Compatible partners are born in the Years of the Horse, Ox, and Snake.

IF YOU ARE SCORPIO BORN IN THE YEAR OF THE DOG

Years of the Dog

1910	1958	2006	2054
1922	1970	2018	2066
1934	1982	2030	2078
1946	1994	2042	2090

The Chinese Dog, like dogs everywhere, is faithful, true, and dedicated, exemplifying the best qualities of devotion. Being able to be counted on runs through your character—and Dog honesty and kindness give your Scorpio tenacity extra capacity for caring. You also have a natural talent for research, business, and making money. You use your Scorpio Dog creativity to solve problems others can't begin to unravel. You're expressive and (though you'd never be called far-out) receptive to experimental ideas. Privately you're a worrier, but outwardly you show confidence. You're very attentive to people's needs, and in fact you must learn to look after yourself as much as you look after others. This is especially true in love; you tend to give more, emotionally and sexually, than you receive. On the other hand, you can be a faultfinder, so beware of shrewish tendencies. Compatible partners are born in the Years of the Rabbit, Dog, Pig, and Tiger.

IF YOU ARE SCORPIO BORN IN THE YEAR OF THE PIG

Ⓧ

Years of the Pig

1911	1959	2007	2055
1923	1971	2019	2067
1935	1983	2031	2079
1947	1995	2043	2091

The Western pig is an object of derision, but the Chinese Pig is chivalrous, elegant, a scholar, and possessor of style and grace. Adding Pig charisma and intelligence to your Scorpio willpower magnifies your persuasive way with people. You're an authority figure with a gallant demeanor and a delightful social touch. You believe in doing your best, and your attention to detail inspires others. In a sense, you're an innocent, for you don't succumb to temptations (e.g., cutting corners, telling white lies). Of course, as a Scorpio you're honest, but as a Scorpio Pig you're more open and up front. In fact, some call you loud and boisterous. Scorpio Pig is also good-looking, and being enchanting and enticing in the love department, you have your share of emotional soap operas. You're very sexual, which arouses lovers' libidos and jealousies. You, yourself, can be too starry-eyed, so choose carefully. Compatible partners are born in the Years of the Rabbit, Dog, Pig, and Tiger.

YOU AND NUMEROLOGY

Numerology is the language of numbers. It is the belief that there is a correlation between numbers and living things, ideas, and concepts. Certainly, numbers surround and infuse our lives (e.g., twenty-four hours in a day, twelve months of the year, etc.). And from ancient times mystics have taught that numbers carry a *vibration*, a deeper meaning that defines how each of us fits into the universe. According to numerology, you are born with a personal number that contains information about who you are and what you need to be happy. This number expresses what numerology calls your life path.

All numbers reduce to one of nine digits, numbers 1 through 9. Your personal number is based on your date of birth. To calculate your number, write your birth date in numerals. As an example, the birth date of October 27, 1981, is written 10-27-1981. Now begin the addition: $10 + 27 + 1 + 9 + 8 + 1 = 56$; 56 reduces to $5 + 6 = 11$; 11 reduces to $1 + 1 = 2$. The personal number for someone born October 27, 1981, is *Two*.

IF YOU ARE A SCORPIO ONE

Keywords: Confidence and Creativity

One is the number of leadership and new beginnings. You enjoy the process of new creation and tend to be more willing to explore than many Scorpios. You're courageous and inventive, and people respond to your decisiveness if not always to your dictatorial ways. You're attracted to unusual pursuits because you like to be one-of-a-kind. You can't bear to be under the thumb of other people's whims and agendas. Careers that call to you are those in which you are in charge and able to work independently. As for love, you want ecstasy and passion and larger-than-life relationships, and you hate the lulls.

IF YOU ARE A SCORPIO TWO

Keywords: Cooperation and Balance

Two is the number of cooperation and creating a secure entity. Being a Two gives you extra Scorpio magnetism—you attract what you need. Your magic is not only your people skills, but also your ability to breathe life into empty forms (e.g., a concept, an ambitious business idea, a new relationship) and produce something of worth. In your work, you need total control and you're a perfectionist—and because you have both a creative side *and* a practical side, you're drawn to careers that combine a business sense with an artistic challenge. In love, your deepest desire is for a loving partnership with someone you can trust and share confidences with.

IF YOU ARE A SCORPIO THREE

Keywords: Expression and Sensitivity

Three symbolizes self-expression. You have a gift for words and a talent for visualization. You link people together so that they benefit from each other—you stimulate others to think. In a career, Scorpio creativity and ability to grasp concepts are your specialties. You're a quick study, mentally active, and you gravitate toward those who can keep up with your rapid thinking. In love you need someone who excites you intellectually and sensually, and understands your complex personality. You don't allow casual acquaintances into your deeper self, but you must have a soulmate with whom you share yourself fully.

IF YOU ARE A SCORPIO FOUR

Keywords: Stability and Process

Four is the number of dedication and loyalty. It represents *foundation*, exactly as a four-sided square does. You are a builder, and the direction you go in is up. First you plan, then day-by-day you add the next step, the next layer, keeping on schedule. You create Scorpio stability by following a process, and your strength is that you're persistent. Therefore, you're able to control your environment, accomplish great works, and achieve high honor. In love, you look for a relationship with staying power. You need a faithful, giving, and understanding lover with whom you can express your intense sensuality.

IF YOU ARE A SCORPIO FIVE

Keywords: Freedom and Discipline

Five is the number of change and freedom. With your chameleon intellect (it can go in any direction) and mesmerizing ability to deal with the public, you're a marvelous *persuader*. You influence others and are a role model. However, as skilled as you are with people, in your own work you stay far away from anyone else's beaten path. You use your inventive mind to push past boundaries, which is how you put Scorpio control on your environment. In love, you need romantic fantasy but also want a partner who looks ahead to new goals. When you give your heart away it's to someone with whom you passionately mesh—body and mind.

IF YOU ARE A SCORPIO SIX

Keywords: Vision and Acceptance

Six is the number of teaching, healing, and utilizing your talents. You're geared toward changing the world or at least fixing other people's lives. Being an advice-giver and even a therapist to your friends comes naturally. You're also competitive, exacting, and demanding—especially with yourself. You're your own harshest critic, for you hold yourself up to a standard of excellence. As a Scorpio *perfector*, you'd like life to run like a well-oiled machine. In love, you're fervent about being a helpmate and confidante, as well as a lover. You're also an intense sensualist who gives your all to someone you trust.

IF YOU ARE A SCORPIO SEVEN

Keywords: Trust and Openness

Seven is the number of the mystic and the intensely focused specialist. You have an instinct for problem-solving, and in a flash understand how things work (in business, between people, etc.). You're an intellectual, a philosopher, and connoisseur of everything creative. With your Scorpio power of organization, you carve out your own territory. Your work, though, is only part of a deeper search for self knowledge. At your core you're extremely loyal and intensely loving, though very selective about relationships. In love, you need a partner brave enough to journey with you in your creation of an *important* life.

IF YOU ARE A SCORPIO EIGHT

Keywords: Abundance and Power

Eight is the number of mastery and authority. You are intelligent, alert, quick in action, born to take power in your own hands and guide traffic into the direction you want. You work well in large groups because you see what's needed and can delegate (a major success tool). Others sense you're the one who knows best, and they're right. You think big, tackle the hard stuff, and never let anyone down. As a Scorpio Eight, you're totally true to your word. Giving your promise in love is a very serious act. You are a protective and deeply caring lover, and in turn you need to know your lover is your unwavering ally.

IF YOU ARE A SCORPIO NINE

Keywords: Integrity and Wisdom

Nine is the path of the "old soul," the number of completion and full bloom. Because it's the last number, it sums up the highs and lows of human experience, and you live a life of dramatic events. You're very intellectual, deeply feeling, extremely protective, interested in all kinds of exploration. People see you as colorful and heroic because you have large ambitions and are also spiritual and altruistic. In love, you're truthful and sincere—a romantic and highly sensual creature who wants to bond closely. As a Scorpio Nine you give generously of yourself, and are an all-protective lover.

LAST WORD: YOUR SCORPIO UNFINISHED BUSINESS

Psychologists often use the phrase *unfinished business* to describe unresolved issues—for example, patterns from childhood that cause unhappiness, anger that keeps one stuck, scenarios of family dysfunction that repeat through second and third generations (such as alcoholism or abusive behavior).

Astrology teaches that the past is indeed very much with us in the present—and that using astrological insights can help us to move out of emotional darkness into greater clarity. Even within this book (which is not a tome of hundreds of pages) you have read of many of the superlatives and challenges of being Scorpio. You have breathtaking gifts and at the same time certain tendencies that can undermine utilizing these abilities.

In nature, a fascinating fact is that in jungles and forests a poisonous plant will grow in a certain spot, and always just a few feet away is a plant that is the antidote to that specific poison. Likewise, in astrology, the antidote is right there ready to be used when the negatives threaten to overwhelm your life.

Scorpio's unfinished business has to do with your emotional depth. Like an iceberg, the visible part of you reveals only a fraction of the whole. Your intense feelings are beneath the surface, and you always have a hidden agenda. Within you swirls a complicated fusion of emotions—thoughts, perceptions, mood swings, yearnings, depression, bouts of loneliness, rage, and longing.

Of course, everyone has feelings and emotions, but Scorpio's seem vaster, deeper, and certainly more intense. And from an early age you learned to manage these often painful feelings by developing a powerful control.

On a psychological level, Scorpio fears helplessness and, even worse, abandonment. The way to keep safe in a chaotic world (both the inner and outer) is to maintain control. You have steely determination to not suffer from your feelings, and many times it's far easier to kill them off rather than endure the intense discomfort of feeling them. Scorpio's symbol is the scorpion, and in real life, when cornered with no escape, this creature will sting itself to death rather than be killed by another.

Your issues center on the fear, rage, and despair you hold inside yourself. You can be very dark. Your moodiness and depression can engulf you. In your mind, you ruminate about a negative event, relive it, take it apart, go round and round, which leads you farther down into a pool of negativity. Scorpio is a manipulator, and your manipulations come back around to you in negative ways. Your dark side can be very self-destructive as well as addictive.

Scorpio is also linked to sex (the act of union and creation), and sex itself, the acting out again and again of intense sexual involvements, can become one of your addictions. If you are wronged by another, your instinct is to get revenge, and you're very capable of exacting vengeance. Power, control, sex, and dark rage produce a dangerous psychological brew.

Yet the antidotes are there to be found in their entirety in being Scorpio, for you have the power of transformation. In addition to being brilliant, gifted, a leader among people, you possess spiritual radiance. Yours is the sign of death and rebirthing, but along with the darkness of the Scorpio experience, you also represent being reborn into the light.

Certainly, death, separations, and endings are an underlying theme in your experience. Many Scorpios lose a significant adult figure in childhood, or undergo a business reversal, or suffer the end of a crucial relationship, or let go of an old way of living and start anew in a completely different setting. The archetypal Scorpionic journey takes you through some kind of emotional death and rebirthing. Through a painful descent, you arise anew. In your real life (rather than in mythic terms), this means that everything you go through, the soap-opera ups and downs of your life, keeps teaching you how strong, loving, accomplished, and unusual you are. Indeed, your life is an inspiration to others. You're probably unaware of how many people you have "rescued."

Of all the signs, Scorpio best understands the meaning of the word *process*—that change takes time. You're born with the ability to lie in a cocoon of "death" and allow change to happen slowly, and then, like the butterfly, finally emerge transformed.

You're a person of boundless potential. You have true valor. You're passionate and compassionate, profound and creative. On the highest level, Scorpio represents the immense powers of the soul. Your unfinished business is to tap into your idealism and utilize your courage—and go through your darkness. On the other side of this valley, you will find authentic security. And with this emotional safety, you can soar like an eagle (another symbol for Scorpio) toward your destiny to change the world.

FAMOUS PEOPLE WITH THE SUN IN SCORPIO

Spiro Agnew
Marie Antoinette
Ed Asner
Christiaan Barnard
Roseanne Barr
Sarah Bernhardt
Edwin Booth
Charles Bronson
Tina Brown
Richard Burton
Laura Bush
Albert Camus
Johnny Carson
James Carville
Dick Cavett
Benvenuto Cellini
Charles, Prince of Wales
Chiang Kai-shek
John Cleese
Michael Crichton
Hillary Rodham Clinton
Barbara Cook
Peter Cook
Stephen Crane
Walter Cronkite
Marie Curie
Rodney Dangerfield
Bo Derek
Danny DeVito
Leonardo DiCaprio
Fyodor Dostoyevsky
Richard Dreyfuss
Sally Field
Jodie Foster
Felix Frankfurter
Indira Gandhi

Bill Gates
Whoopi Goldberg
Ruth Gordon
Billy Graham
Ken Griffey Jr.
Moss Hart
Harry Hamlin
Goldie Hawn
Shere Hite
Bob Hoskins
Rock Hudson
Mahalia Jackson
Peter Jackson
James Jones
George S. Kaufman
John Keats
Grace Kelly
Robert Kennedy
Larry King
Calvin Klein
Kevin Kline
Hedy Lamarr
Burt Lancaster
k. d. lang
Fran Lebowitz
Vivien Leigh
Martin Luther
Charles Manson
Joseph McCarthy
Joni Mitchell
Margaret Mitchell
François Mitterand
Claude Monet
Demi Moore
Mike Nichols
Georgia O'Keeffe

George Patton
Joaquin Phoenix
Pablo Picasso
Sylvia Plath
Emily Post
Ezra Pound
Claude Rains
Dan Rather
Ann Reinking
Condoleezza Rice
Julia Roberts
Auguste Rodin
Roy Rogers
Will Rogers
Theodore Roosevelt
Hermann Rorschach
Meg Ryan
Winona Ryder
Carl Sagan
Jonas Salk
Martin Scorsese
Maria Shriver
Grace Slick
Robert Louis Stevenson
Lee Strasberg
Billy Sunday
Joan Sutherland
Dylan Thomas
Leon Trotsky
Ted Turner
Voltaire
Kurt Vonnegut
Sam Waterston
Stanford White
Owen Wilson

PART TWO

ALL ABOUT YOUR SIGN OF SCORPIO

SCORPIO'S ASTROLOGICAL AFFINITIES, LINKS, AND LORE

SYMBOL: The Scorpion

A secretive, deadly creature that can poison its enemies. Its sting is often fatal. In ancient Egypt, the scorpion goddess, Selket, wielded lethal power over her enemies but also used her power to protect. Paintings and sculptures of Selket were placed in coffins and tombs; she was shown with her arms extended in a protective gesture to welcome the dead. In Hindu belief, the scorpion opens the doorway to the next world.

RULING PLANET: Pluto ♇

Ancient god of the netherworld and of the dead. In Greek mythology, three gods (who were brothers) ruled over the three realms of the cosmos. Pluto was sovereign of the underworld, Zeus was God of the Heavens, and Poseidon reigned over the seas. In astrology, Pluto rules regenerative forces and the beginnings and ends of phases in life. Pluto represents something going out of existence and a new order coming into being.

DOMINANT KEYWORD

I DESIRE

GLYPH ♏

The pictograph is the stinger of the Scorpion connected to a representation of the human reproductive organs (the part of the anatomy that Scorpio rules). This was the symbol in ancient times for the phoenix, bird of immortality and regeneration. In symbolic terms, the curved lines and arrow represent strong emotions tied to practicality and aiming toward higher consciousness.

PART OF THE BODY RULED BY SCORPIO:
The Genitals

Scorpio people are susceptible to infections of the urinary system and venereal disease. In addition, their volatile emotions are often the cause of exhaustion and ill health.

LUCKY DAY: Tuesday

The day named for Mars, which in classical astrology was the ruler of Scorpio. *Tiw* is the Old English name for Mars, and Tuesday comes from *Tiwesdaeg*, meaning Tiw's Day.

After 1930, when the planet Pluto was discovered, Pluto became Scorpio's planetary ruler. When a new planet is discovered—and studied by the astrological community—the new planet is assigned to a zodiac sign as its ruler. The three modern planets are Uranus, which after 1781 became the ruler of Aquarius; Neptune, which after 1846 became the ruler of Pisces; and Pluto, which after 1930 became the ruler of Scorpio.

LUCKY NUMBERS: 2 and 4

Numerologically, 2 is the number of germination, wisdom, insight, and persuasion—and 4 is linked to dedication, discipline, keeping order, and the ability to endure. These themes align with the nature of Scorpio.

TAROT CARD: Death

The card in the Tarot linked to Scorpio is Death. An ancient name for this card is Child of the Great Transformer. The Death card tends to stir up alarm, but it should not be feared, for its message is positive. It symbolizes metamorphosis, transformation, birth, and renewal. In the Tarot, the card speaks of the start of a new experience and triumph in the undertaking. The Death card points to something that has run its course and says the ending will lead to a beginning. When this card turns up in a Tarot reading, the advice is to not fear letting go of what is used up—for this comes at the right moment to provide you with freedom to create something new.

The card itself pictures a dark skeleton wearing a suit of armor who rides a white horse heading toward the rising sun. The Horseman carries a banner emblazoned with the five-petaled Mystic Rose that signifies life. The symbolism is that life constantly changes from the old to the new.

For Scorpio, the message of the Death Tarot card is that deep within you, you know that everything in life must change and evolve. It tells you to relinquish the worthless so you can discover your true treasure. By mastering your passions and negative behavior, Scorpio, you free your creative imagination and your power to love.

MAGICAL BIRTHSTONE: Topaz

A gemstone that comes in many hues, but is best known for a fiery golden-amber color. The word *topaz* comes from the Sanskrit, meaning "the subject of the search" and also "fire"; the stone is symbolic of something hard to find. It is said to come from Topazos, an island named for the Greek word for "conjecture" (*topazein*). Legend has it the topaz is one of the gemstones that form the foundation to the twelve gates to the Holy City of Jerusalem. In ancient times, the topaz was used as an amulet to protect from illness, cool fevers, and defend against enemies. During the

Middle Ages it was touched to the skin of plague victims in the belief it would cure ulcers and blisters. For Scorpio, the topaz is said to release occult powers, calm frayed tempers and high passions, heal sadness, and bring serenity of mind.

SPECIAL COLORS

Crimson, Deep Red, Burgundy, Maroon: The glowing colors of passion.

CONSTELLATION OF SCORPIO

Scorpius (also known as Scorpio, the Latin word for "scorpion") is one of the brightest, most recognizable constellations in the sky. More than any other constellation, it resembles its given name. It contains a red supergiant star, Antares, known as the Heart of the Scorpion. The Babylonians called this constellation "Creature with a Burning Sting." In ancient China, this star-grouping was known as a Dragon, and in ancient India as the Dark Serpent. The Greek myth around this constellation has to do with Orion, the great hunter, who boasted he could slay any beast. The gods taught Orion a lesson by sending a scorpion to sting his foot, thus killing him. Both Orion and the scorpion were placed into the heavens, but to prevent them from fighting, they were put on opposite sides of the sky. The two constellations are never visible at the same time—Orion shines in winter, and the Scorpion in summer, and when one rises, the other sets.

CITIES

Liverpool, New Orleans, Washington, D.C., Newcastle

COUNTRIES

Algeria, Morocco, Tahiti, Norway

FLOWERS

Chrysanthemum, Rhododendron, and Geranium

TREES

Blackthorn and other bushy tress

HERBS AND SPICES

Witch Hazel, Aloes, and Catmint

METAL: Plutonium

A silvery-white radioactive metal with a high rate of spontaneous fission. It was discovered and isolated in 1940, and first used in quantity during World War II to build the atomic bombs that were dropped on the Japanese cities of Hiroshima and Nagasaki.

In recent years, plutonium has been used in medicine (radiation), in engineering, and to fuel rocket ships and space probes. Plutonium's ability to destroy as well as its positive use in nuclear medicine and as nuclear power aligns with the qualities of Scorpio.

ANIMALS RULED BY SCORPIO

Insects and Crustaceans

DANGER

Scorpio's nature is to dominate and control, which quickly gives rise to resentment in others. In relationships, Scorpio's secretiveness and jealousy provoke anger in those close to you. Scorpio also has a sharp, stinging temper that can enrage others to the point of violence.

PERSONAL PROVERBS

It is only when the heavens are dark that one can see the stars.

Change is not something you do; it is something you allow.

KEYWORDS FOR SCORPIO

Powerful intellect

Complex

Leader

Capable

Practical

Curious

Loyal

Possessive

Intense

Passionate

Sexually torrid

Stubborn

Exacting

Nonconforming

Healer

Mystical

Psychic

Secretive

Obsessive

Dictatorial

Arrogant

Manipulative

Vindictive

Lonely

Self-destructive

Unusual destiny

Goes through turning points that lead to rebirth

HOW ASTROLOGY SLICES AND DICES YOUR SIGN OF SCORPIO

DUALITY: Feminine

The twelve astrological signs are divided into two groups, *masculine* and *feminine*. Six are masculine and six are feminine; this is known as the sign's *duality*. A masculine sign is direct and energetic. A feminine sign is receptive and magnetic. These attributes were given to the signs about 2,500 years ago. Today modern astrologers avoid the sexism implicit in these distinctions. A masculine sign does not mean "positive and forceful" any more than a feminine sign means "negative and weak." In modern terminology, the masculine signs are defined as outer-directed and strong through action. The feminine signs, such as your sign of Scorpio, are self-contained and strong through inner reserves.

TRIPLICITY (ELEMENT): Water

The twelve signs are also divided into groups of three signs each. These three-sign groups are called a *triplicity*, and each of these denotes an *element*. The elements are *Fire*, *Earth*, *Air*, and *Water*. In astrology, an element symbolizes a fundamental characterization of the sign.

The three *Fire* signs are Aries, Leo, and Sagittarius. Fire signs are active and enthusiastic.

The three *Earth* signs are Taurus, Virgo, and Capricorn. Earth signs are practical and stable.

The three *Air* signs are Gemini, Libra, and Aquarius. Air signs are intellectual and communicative.

The three *water* signs are Cancer, Scorpio, and Pisces. Water signs are emotional and intuitive.

QUADRUPLICITY (QUALITY): Fixed

The twelve signs are also divided into groups of four signs each. These four-sign groups are called a *quadruplicity*, and each of these denotes a *quality*. The qualities are *Cardinal*, *Fixed*, and *Mutable*. In astrology, the quality signifies the sign's interaction with the outside world.

Four signs are *Cardinal** signs. They are Aries, Cancer, Libra, and Capricorn. Cardinal signs are enterprising and outgoing. They are the initiators and leaders.

Four signs are *Fixed*. They are Taurus, Leo, Scorpio, and Aquarius. Fixed signs are resistant to change. They hold on; they're perfectors and finishers, rather than originators.

---

*When the Sun crosses the four cardinal points in the zodiac, we mark the beginning of each of our four seasons. Aries begins spring; Cancer begins summer; Libra begins fall; Capricorn begins winter.

Four signs are *Mutable*. They are Gemini, Virgo, Sagittarius, and Pisces. Mutable signs are flexible, versatile, and adaptable. They are able to adjust to differing circumstances.

Your sign of Scorpio is a Feminine, Water, Fixed sign—and no other sign in the zodiac is this exact combination. Your sign is a one-of-a-kind combination, and therefore you express the characteristics of your duality, element, and quality differently from any other sign.

For example, your sign is a *Feminine* sign, meaning you are receptive, caring, protective, and resourceful. You're a *Water* sign, meaning you're creative, imaginative, deeply feeling, and intuitive. And you're a *Fixed* sign, meaning you're dedicated, committed, resolute, and persistent, and you hold on tenaciously.

Now, the sign of Cancer is also Feminine and Water, but unlike Scorpio (which is Fixed), Cancer is Cardinal. Like you, Cancer is a nurturer and life-giver who is loyal, devoted, gifted creatively, and wise about the human heart—but Cancer is quick to go after opportunity, especially if it promises greater gain. Cancer is committed but doesn't have quite your intense staying power (few do). Unlike you, Cancer will abandon a project for another, especially if motivated by more money. You, being Fixed, stay the course to your final goal. You won't be diverted by easy promises; you're there to the finish.

Pisces, too, is Feminine and Water, but unlike Scorpio (which is Fixed), Pisces is Mutable. Like you, Pisces is intuitive, inspirational, and deeply creative, in tune with emotions and things unseen. However, being Mutable, Pisces is also variable, up-and-down. Pisces is easily sidetracked, distractible, and drifts in the direction the current takes it. Pisces wants to escape. You, on the other hand, are Fixed, and aren't subject to the vagaries of others.

You have clear objectives and are focused on your commitments. When you feel you're in the right, you're immovable.

POLARITY: Taurus

The twelve signs are also divided into groups of two signs each. These two-sign groups are called a *polarity* (meaning "opposite"). Each sign in the zodiac has a polarity, which is its opposite sign in the other half of the zodiac. The two signs express opposite characteristics.

Scorpio and Taurus are a polarity. Scorpio is the sign of emotional, mental, and physical regeneration. The themes of transformation and rebirth run through your experiences. You're the sign of intensity, willpower, passion, knowledge, and high achievement. Scorpio also represents "inheritance from the past," which encompasses not only financial gain through others, but the psychological gains that empower you as you evolve. You're born with a sense of purpose and destiny, and the issues you absorb from childhood give you depth of understanding. You possess immense emotional strength you can use to help others. On an esoteric level, Scorpio is the sign of karma—the principle of "you reap what you sow."

Taurus, your opposite sign, is the sign of money and values. It symbolizes possessions, material wealth, and creating security. Taurus is rooted in practicality and being down-to-earth—its natives feel comfortable in the familiar and what has stood the test of time. In work, Taurus has an affinity for building and growing. He or she tends to think in concrete terms and likes to deal with what is tangible and "real." There's something pure and basic about Taurus.

Astrologically, you as a Scorpio can benefit from adopting some of Taurus's uncomplicated approach. Scorpio can get very convoluted. In your labyrinthine way, you start digging deeper, figure out everyone's motivation, and look for how you can sway the outcome of a situation. You don't have a simple mind, and therefore no circumstance is ever simple. You and Taurus both seek security, but Taurus's method is to gather up worldly goods and hold family and friends near. Yours is to control, not only your own environment but other people's as well. Taurus is known for pragmatism and common sense. And taking on more of this matter-of-fact, it-is-what-it-is attitude can spare you from constantly defending yourself from possible emotional harm. You can relax more, let go of some of your painful intensity.

In turn, Taurus has lessons to learn from you: One is to see things in a new way. Taurus can become far more stuck than you in a nonproductive pattern. You, having powers to transform, ride through personal shifts more gracefully. Another lesson to take from you is to learn from experience. Taurus becomes attached to an opinion and, despite the outcome, won't let go of the idea that *that's* the way it has to be. Thus, Taurus perpetuates its struggle. It can benefit from Scorpio's ability to see the subtleties of emotional situations, and adjust to these. Finally, Taurus needs to put less importance on material things than on the deeper verities of character. Taurus will often judge others by outward success rather than look into another's heart.

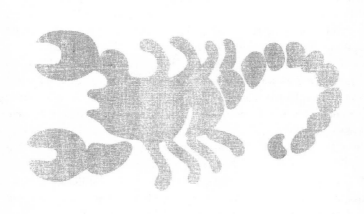